border to border · teen to teen · border to border · teen to teen · border to border

TEENS IN CHINA

Teens in China

China

by Karen Elizabeth Conyers

Content Adviser: Cynthia Ning, Ph.D.,
Associate Director, Center For Chinese Studies,
University of Hawaii

Reading Adviser: Peggy Ballard, Ph.D.,
Department of Educational Studies,
Minnesota State University, Mankato

Compass Point Books ◆ Minneapolis, Minnesota

Compass Point Books
3109 West 50th Street, #115
Minneapolis, MN 55410

Editor: Shelly Lyons
Designers: The Design Lab and Jaime Martens
Page Production: Bobbie Nyutten and Ashlee Schultz
Photo Researcher: The Design Lab
Geographic Researcher: Lisa Thornquist, Ph.D.
Cartographer: XNR Productions, Inc.
Library Consultant: Kathleen Baxter

Art Director: Jaime Martens
Creative Director: Keith Griffin
Editorial Director: Carol Jones
Managing Editor: Catherine Neitge

*I would like to dedicate this book to my husband, Dan, and my sons, Michael, Andrew, and
Eric. Without their unflagging love and support, this project would not have been possible.
KEC*

Library of Congress Cataloging-in-Publication Data
Conyers, Karen Elizabeth.
Teens in China / by Karen Elizabeth Conyers.
   p. cm.—(Global connections)
   Includes bibliographical references and index.
   ISBN-13: 978-0-7565-2060-1 (library binding)
   ISBN-10: 0-7565-2060-6 (library binding)
   ISBN-13: 978-0-7565-2068-7 (paperback)
   ISBN-10: 0-7565-2068-1 (paperback)
   1. Teenagers—Asia—Social conditions. 2. Teenagers—Asia—Conduct of life. I. Title.
II. Series.
   HQ799.A75.C66 2007
   305.2350951—dc22   2006027053

Visit Compass Point Books on the Internet at www.compasspointbooks.com
or e-mail your request to custserv@compasspointbooks.com.

Table of Contents

Beijing

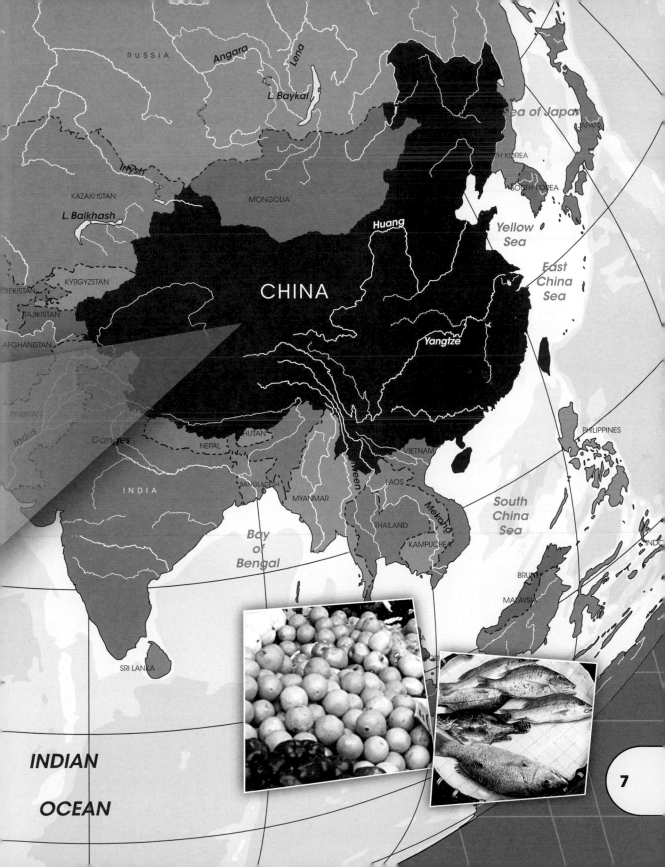

RUSSIA

Angara

Lena

L. Baykal

Sea of Japan

JAPAN

KAZAKHSTAN

MONGOLIA

NORTH KOREA

SOUTH KOREA

L. Balkhash

Huang

Yellow
Sea

KYRGYZSTAN

East
China
Sea

UZBEKISTAN

TAJIKISTAN

CHINA

AFGHANISTAN

Yangtze

Indus

PAKISTAN

Ganges

BHUTAN

NEPAL

Ween

VIETNAM

PHILIPPINES

INDIA

BANGLADESH

LAOS

MYANMAR

South
China
Sea

THAILAND

Mekong

KAMPUCHEA

INDO

Bay
of
Bengal

BRUNEI

MALAYSIA

SRI LANKA

INDIAN

OCEAN

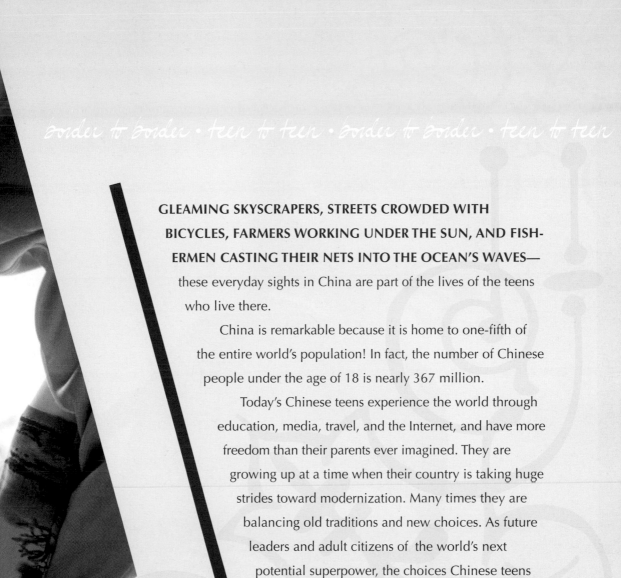

GLEAMING SKYSCRAPERS, STREETS CROWDED WITH BICYCLES, FARMERS WORKING UNDER THE SUN, AND FISHERMEN CASTING THEIR NETS INTO THE OCEAN'S WAVES— these everyday sights in China are part of the lives of the teens who live there.

China is remarkable because it is home to one-fifth of the entire world's population! In fact, the number of Chinese people under the age of 18 is nearly 367 million.

Today's Chinese teens experience the world through education, media, travel, and the Internet, and have more freedom than their parents ever imagined. They are growing up at a time when their country is taking huge strides toward modernization. Many times they are balancing old traditions and new choices. As future leaders and adult citizens of the world's next potential superpower, the choices Chinese teens make will have impact worldwide.

9

China's Ministry of Education has recently committed to focusing on balancing the education of China's rural and urban teens. The Chinese government hopes there will be equal opportunities for all Chinese youth to succeed in the future.

1

Academic Discipline

SCHOOL IS PERHAPS the most important task of every child in China today. There is tremendous pressure for teens to succeed in school. Because the government only allows couples to have one child, parents often pin all of their hopes for the future on their child. For Chinese teens, doing well in school means the possibility of reaching financial well-being, often for their entire family. The Chinese government also pushes students by teaching them that it is their duty to work hard and learn well, so they can contribute their skills to the nation and ensure China's prosperity.

For most of China's history, only males from important families received an education. During the last century, though, things began to change, and education became more available to

Teen Scenes

A 15-year-old boy wakes up to the sound of his mother's voice.

After throwing on some clothes, he eats a quick breakfast of *congee*, or rice porridge, and green tea. Next, he feeds the chickens and helps his father fix a piece of machinery.

congee
kon-GEE

Once his chores are completed, it's time for school, so he grabs his books and begins his 2-mile (3.2-kilometer) walk. He meets a friend along the way and they talk anxiously about the math test they will take later that day.

At school, their crowded classroom fills with students, all of whom live near the small town where the school is located. They stand and sing the Chinese national anthem. Shortly after they begin working on their math exam.

After school the boy joins a group of friends as they all make their way home. There are five of them, but only three will continue school after this year. He hopes to continue his studies at a vocational school training for a career as a manager. One day he will have a successful career at the new automotive manufacturing plant that is being built near his school.

Another 15-year-old teen, a girl living in Beijing, wakes up to the sound of her alarm clock blaring the latest pop tune by her favorite musician, Jay Chow. She slides out of bed and searches for her jeans and a shirt.

Breakfast consists of a quick pastry and a small cup of green tea. Her father walks into the kitchen and kisses her on the forehead. Her mother follows closely behind. The three of them grab their bags and walk out the door. The elevator ride down from their 10th-story apartment seems long today. Her parents drive her to school, where she sees her group of friends gathered in the yard.

The students sing the national anthem and then begin their daily English lesson.

After school, she joins her friends at a popular Internet cafe, where they will play games and e-mail acquaintances. As they walk to the cafe, they talk about their plans for the future. All of them will continue their educations at a senior middle school next year, and in just a few years they will all take the college entrance exam. Only one out of five is likely to make it into a Chinese university. The girl hopes it will be her, because her dreams of becoming a doctor depend on it.

Her parents pick her up from the cafe, and the three of them head home. After a long day, they decide to pick up dinner at their favorite fast-food restaurant.

Traditional and modern Chinese teens living in different areas grow up with varying experiences and have different dreams.

the common people. In 1978, Chinese officials adopted a policy that required all students to complete a minimum of nine years of school, beginning with elementary school at age 6.

Before elementary school, most Chinese youngsters attend all-day pre-school, or kindergarten, for one to three years. In preschool, they sing, dance, play games, and develop their language skills. Through stories and games, they also begin to learn important lessons, such as being truthful, kind, and polite.

In elementary school, children study Chinese language, math, science, arts, physical education, and moral education, such as the teachings of the famous Chinese thinker Confucius. Most important at this age is language, as they learn how to read and write Chinese characters.

Mandarin Chinese is the official language in China, although there are eight official dialects used among the different ethnic groups. All of these dialects share the same written language, so even if people can't understand one another's speech, they can still communicate in writing. Pinyin is the phonetic spelling system that uses the Roman alphabet to spell Chinese names and geographic locations.

In 2004, China's government spent just 2.79 percent of the country's gross domestic product on education. But China's government has recently decided to guarantee more funds for education.

School Life

Most classes in China are large, with as many as 50 students in each, so teachers use lectures to present information. In many schools, there is little opportunity for class discussion or interaction during lessons, but interactive instruction is growing in popularity. Students are required to memorize information for tests. Teachers grade the tests using percentage points. Many students feel pressure from their parents to achieve high grades, and there is a lot of competition to be the best in the class.

In most schools, students wear uniforms, such as black pants and white shirts or blue warm up suits. However, a growing number of urban schools have done away with uniforms, allowing students more individuality. Teens are enthusiastic about being able to select their own outfits for school. In cities, especially, many teens are fashion-conscious and have trendy clothing and hairstyles, and the girls wear makeup. In rural areas, though, there tends to be less variety. Loose pants, long shirts, and sandals are the norm for most daily activities, and uniforms are required at schools.

Chinese schools reward both academic ability and good character. The best elementary school students receive green ties from the school to wear with their uniforms in recognition of their success. All children eventually receive ties, but the best students are honored first.

The school year begins in early September and lasts until late June. Students attend school five days a week, from 8 A.M. until 4:30 or 5 P.M. Each morning, students gather outside their

Chinese Characters

Chinese characters are ideographs—symbols that convey a meaning. This type of writing has been in existence for more than 3,000 years. Most Chinese characters are made up of a meaning component and a sound component, and it usually takes two characters to make a Chinese word. The sequence one uses to make the strikes is also important. Texts can be written and read from top to bottom, from right to left, or from left to right. Most modern texts are written from left to right.

人	天	福
MAN	SKY	LUCK

Elite private schools exist in China, and mainly upper-income families can afford their fees of around 50,000 yuan (U.S.$6,385) per year.

schools to raise the red and yellow flag, sing the Chinese national anthem, and do group exercises before class. In most rural areas, there are not enough teachers. Many have moved away to teach in large cities, where schools offer better financial and educational opportunities. Math, history, art, science, languages, and physical education are taught in crowded classrooms.

When it's lunchtime, rice and vegetables are on the menu. A two-hour break allows time for recess and a nap or studying before afternoon classes begin. At the end of the school day, most students attend programs until their parents are finished with work. Some teens go to recreation centers where they build model airplanes, write stories, perform in plays, or learn computer skills. Others

A group of students in Hong Kong gather at school to study together.

participate in team sports such as soccer or basketball.

Teachers assign several hours of homework each night, especially once students reach middle school. In some communities, students return to school several nights each week and sometimes even on Saturdays to do homework. This is especially true for city kids living in very small apartments—it's easier to use the desks and books at school than to try to find a good spot at home. Teachers are there to help, too, if needed. Students are expected to work hard—and they do—because they hope their hard work will lead to high scores on the college entrance exam. For Chinese teens, this exam is the focus of their schooling. Most of their classes are structured around what they will be tested on. For teens, this exam is the key to entrance into a respected university.

Junior & Senior Middle School

During the three years of junior middle school, from ages 12 to 15, students take classes in the sciences—such as biology, chemistry, and physics—as well as in geography, history, politics, physical education, and foreign languages. English is the most common foreign language spoken in China today, although other Asian languages, such as Japanese and Korean, are growing in popularity. Moral lessons are also taught, and they focus on Communist ideology, as well as how to be a good Chinese citizen.

When junior middle school ends, students must make an important decision: whether to go to senior middle school for more academic study or attend vocational-technical school to learn a trade. Some students will choose not to do

Internet access is available in about 6 percent of primary schools and about 20 percent of junior middle schools.

Science & Math Classes

Chinese students in grades seven through nine are required to take two years each of biology, chemistry, and physics. Students in grades 10 and 11 are expected to take six credits in each of these three subjects, but additional optional science classes are also offered. The required high school science classes cover homeostasis and the environment, heredity and evolution, and molecular and cellular biology. The optional classes cover modern biological science, biology and society, and biotechnology and practice.

Mathematics classes are also required throughout middle school and high school. The classes cover such specific subjects as elementary solid and plane analytic geometry, elementary statistics and probability, functions and plane vectors, and number sequences and inequalities.

either, and they will work instead.

Most of the country's rural workers—about 480 million people—have a junior middle school education or less. About half of the 16 million students who graduate from junior middle school each year cannot go to senior middle school because of a lack of classrooms and teachers in rural areas. In these places, only the best students are allowed to continue their education.

From 2006 to 2010, the Chinese government is expected to spend 218 billion yuan (U.S.$27.84 billion) to improve education. In the western and central regions of the country the government will build new schools and hire more teachers. In 2006, China began providing free education, books, and uniforms to impoverished rural students in an effort to overcome the education gap between urban and rural citizens. By 2010, all Chinese students will receive their compulsory education at no charge, according to China's Ministry of Education. Previously, the cost of school per year was around 1592 yuan (U.S.$203), which could be more than a rural family's income of 796 to 3183 yuan (U.S.$102 to $406) per year, forcing them into debt.

Vocational-technical training is the most common path chosen by students who live in or near small industrial cities, where trained workers and managers are needed. In 2003, more than 12 million people—about 40 percent of all senior middle school students—were

Children in rural areas often live with relatives when their parents leave to work in the city. These children—almost 23 million—often lack good education because the schools they attend are underfunded.

enrolled in vocational-technical schools. Teens who decide to go to these schools spend two to four years learning skills they can use in the workforce. Some of the most common industries in China are steel manufacturing, coal mining, cement and fertilizer

Youth Literacy Rate Since 1980

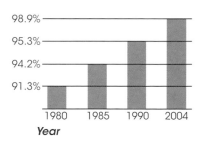

98.9%			
95.3%			
94.2%			
91.3%			
1980	1985	1990	2004

Year

Source: U.N. Common Database.

production, and household appliance manufacturing. A growing industry is automobile manufacturing.

Senior middle school is a continuation of the courses taught in junior middle school. However, now students must decide whether to pursue the sciences, such as chemistry or biology, or the humanities, such as language or social studies. Their classes are tailored to those interests. Each year, senior middle schools hold contests that allow the students to compete in their subjects, helping them to prepare for the national college entrance exams.

Higher Education

Students who successfully complete senior middle school can apply to college after taking one of two national college entrance exams—in engineering and the sciences, or in arts and humanities. These three-day exams occur in early July. Because of the difficulty of the exams and the terribly hot weather, students have nicknamed this time period "Black July."

The exams determine which

In 2006, 88 million students took the college entrance exams; of these, 9.52 million applied for just 2.6 million undergraduate openings.

Graduation Ceremonies

Graduation ceremonies are held for students finishing elementary, junior, and senior middle schools. As each graduate's name is announced to the group, a school official presents the student with a certificate of achievement. A teacher mentions some of the student's special traits, such as being talented in math, or a hard worker. After the ceremony, at some schools, the graduates ask friends and teachers to write blessings in their yearbooks. Celebrations are usually family affairs, focused on the students' academic success.

High school graduates at Heifei No. 1 High School in eastern China throw their mortarboards in celebration.

students will attend one of the 2,000 colleges and universities in China. In 2002, these institutions had a total of 9 million students. By 2005, the total number of students had risen to 20 million, but the number of universities remained the same. Even so, this increase in enrollment lags behind the number of students actually hoping to attend.

It is not just academic ability that determines admission. Students are also judged on physical ability, moral character, and social behavior, which admission officers determine through background checks.

Senior middle school students who are selected for one of China's colleges or universities will spend four years working toward a bachelor's degree. College students can study

Hong Kong Polytechnic University is one of 2,000 universities in China.

香港理工大學

THE HONG KONG POLYTECHNIC UNIVERSITY

ACADEMIC DISCIPLINE

nearly any subject, but they are guided toward majors that will most benefit China's future, such as engineering, science, computer science, business, and architecture. Some universities are quite specialized, as noted by their names: Beijing University of Chinese Medicine, the University of Petroleum, the China Agriculture University, the Central Academy of Drama, East China University of Science and Technology, Nanjing University of Aeronautics and Astronautics, and the Ocean University of China.

Students who are interested in military careers can apply to one of the People's Liberation Army (PLA) military academies, which focus on specialized skills training for future officers.

Some students are more interested in secretarial training, fashion design, allied health (medical assistants, lab technicians, X ray technologists, and physical therapists), forestry, or technology. Colleges that offer these two-to-three year programs award diplomas, but not bachelor's degrees.

Typical university charges are at least 8,000 yuan (U.S.$1,022) per year for undergraduate education, which includes a room in the on-campus dormitories. This sum exceeds the annual income of most families in China, so many students must pursue academic scholarships, loans, and part-time employment.

Universities Overseas

If their parents can afford it, many teens will go to foreign countries for their college education. In the past, once the students left, there was little chance they would return to China and their families. Economic opportunities were better overseas in western Europe, Australia, Canada, and the United States. However, as China's economic development improves, more students say they are willing to return. In 2005, about 27,000 students returned to China after completing their college education overseas.

Today about 40 percent of teens in China live in urban areas.

2 Dawn Rising

AT DAWN, THE SUN peeks over the horizon in the rolling countryside of central China, and families begin getting ready for the day. After morning chores and breakfast, the roads fill with bicycles—the most common mode of transportation—as people ride to work and school.

In the capital city of Beijing, the skyscrapers cast long shadows as the sun rises. People wake up to begin the day. Soon the streets fill with buses, motorbikes, cars, and bicycles as people head to their morning destinations.

Nearly 60 percent of Chinese live in small rural communities, where they work in factories or raise animals and crops. While cities such as Hong Kong, Shanghai, and Beijing are bustling with people, the

25

distribution of China's population is uneven. In Shanghai there are, on average, 6,615 people per square mile (2,646 per square km), while the rugged mountains and plateaus of Tibet average only five people per square mile (two per square km).

China is a country of mountains and hills. Only 15 percent of the land can be planted with crops such as wheat, corn, rice, and sweet potatoes.

Most rural families raise animals, such as pigs and chickens, and just enough produce to feed their families. Chinese teens help their parents plow the dirt, haul manure, and harvest ripe crops. The use of irrigation and fertilizers has helped to increase crop production, which allows farm families to earn more money, but those techniques have resulted in soil erosion and pollution. Because of the required physical labor

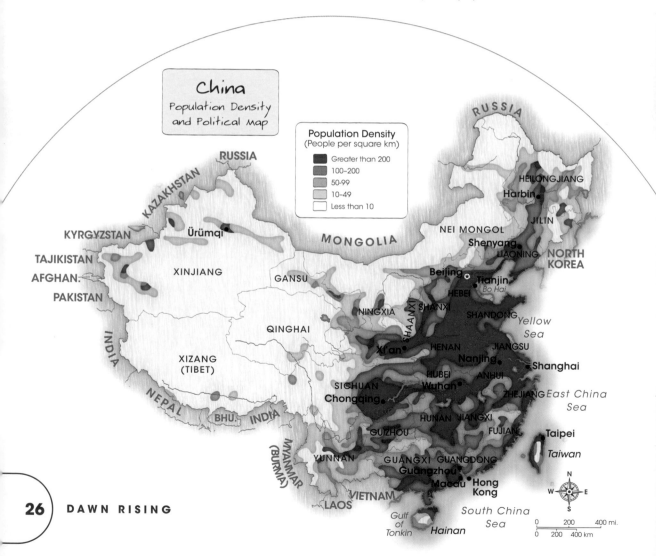

China
Population Density
and Political Map

Population Density
(People per square km)

Greater than 200
100–200
50-99
10–49
Less than 10

RUSSIA

KAZAKHSTAN

KYRGYZSTAN

TAJIKISTAN

AFGHAN.

PAKISTAN

INDIA

NEPAL

BHU.

INDIA

Ürümqi

XINJIANG

GANSU

QINGHAI

XIZANG
(TIBET)

MYANMAR
(BURMA)

YUNNAN

VIETNAM

LAOS

Gulf
of
Tonkin

Hainan

RUSSIA

MONGOLIA

NEI MONGOL

Shenyang

LIAONING

Beijing

Tianjin
Bo Hai

HEBEI

NINGXIA

SHANXI

SHAANXI

SHANDONG

Yellow
Sea

Xi'an

HENAN

JIANGSU

Nanjing

HUBEI

ANHUI

Shanghai

SICHUAN

Wuhan

ZHEJIANG

East China
Sea

Chongqing

HUNAN

JIANGXI

FUJIAN

GUIZHOU

Taipei

Taiwan

GUANGXI

GUANGDONG

Guangzhou

Macau

Hong
Kong

South China
Sea

HEILONGJIANG

Harbin

JILIN

NORTH
KOREA

N
W   E
S

0   200   400 mi.

0   200   400 km

Traditional houses are found in a mountain village in Yunnan Province.

and lack of income, life is difficult for those who live in the country, and many young people—even teenagers—decide to leave home and move to the cities to try to find a better life.

In rural communities, children, their parents, and grandparents usually live together in small homes. Traditional Chinese homes are built of wood with clay tile roofs, although in rural areas some are constructed with mud. Four buildings surround an outdoor courtyard to form a *siheyuan*, or quadrangle. It can only be entered through a single

siheyuan
szz-huh-YEARN

gate at the southwest corner or from the homes themselves. This layout offers privacy and safety to the people who live there. Usually the home is occupied by several generations of a single family. The secluded courtyard, planted with trees and flowers, is a place for family members to meet, do household chores, or relax and play. All of a house's windows face the courtyard; there are no windows on the outside walls.

These traditional homes are always built with an odd number of sections, because in China an even number of sections is considered unlucky. Colorful screens divide the sections into rooms. In a typical three-section house, the

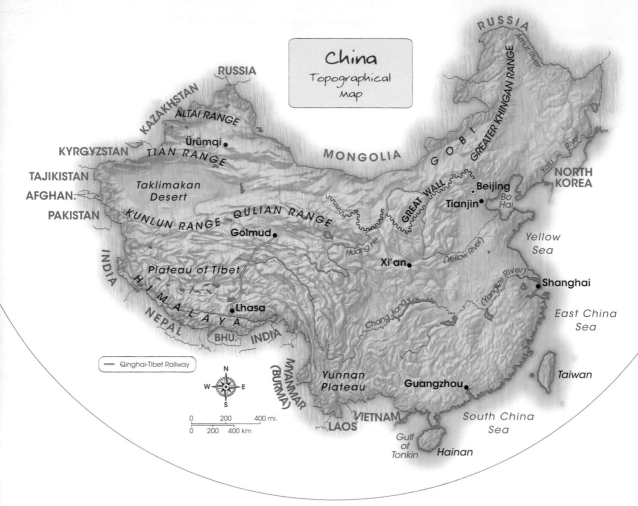

China
Topographical Map

RUSSIA

KAZAKHSTAN

ALTAI RANGE

Ürümqi

TIAN RANGE

KYRGYZSTAN

TAJIKISTAN

AFGHAN.

PAKISTAN

Taklimakan Desert

KUNLUN RANGE

QULIAN RANGE

Golmud

Plateau of Tibet

INDIA

HIMALAYA

NEPAL

BHU.

INDIA

Lhasa

MYANMAR (BURMA)

Qinghai-Tibet Railway

Yunnan Plateau

VIETNAM

LAOS

Gulf of Tonkin

Hainan

MONGOLIA

GOBI

GREATER KHINGAN RANGE

RUSSIA

Amur River

GREAT WALL

Yalu River

NORTH KOREA

Beijing

Tianjin

Bo Hai

Huang He

Xi'an

(Yellow River)

(Yangtze River)

Chang Jiang

Guangzhou

Yellow Sea

Shanghai

East China Sea

Taiwan

South China Sea

N W E S

0   200   400 mi.
0   200   400 km

main room contains the cooking area and a small shrine to the family's ancestors. The other sections are used for sleeping.

In many larger communities, traditional Chinese homes are being replaced with new, modern housing options. In Beijing, Shanghai, and Hong Kong, skyscrapers are being built to accommodate the millions of residents. In these cities, people live in apartment buildings, ride buses or subways to work

and school, and eat at McDonald's. In the most crowded areas of Shanghai, it's not unusual for apartment dwellers to have to share a bathroom or kitchen with their neighbors, because space is so limited.

Teens and young adults who live in cities may meet at Internet cafés after work, go to the movies, or join their friends at clubs to dance and sing karaoke on the weekends.

Internet cafes are popular hangouts for teens who live in large cities.

Daily Routines

No matter where a person lives, daily routines are virtually the same. For teens in China, the day begins at dawn. After waking up and getting dressed, teens do their morning chores, such as fixing the family's morning meal, sweeping the street, or feeding the animals.

After chores *zao can*, or breakfast, is served. A typical breakfast includes congee, or rice porridge, or noodles with shrimp and vegetables. Delicious crullers— long, twisted strips of dough that are deep-

zao can
ZOW SAHN

Time Zone

Although China is wide enough to cover five time zones, all Chinese clocks are set to the same time. According to government policy, everyone operates according to the time in Beijing, the capital city. That means that if you live in Hong Kong, on the eastern edge of China, and your clock says 7 A.M., the sun is rising and so are residents there. But at 7 A.M. in Kashgar, on the far western border, it looks like the middle of the night. The sun won't rise for hours.

fried in hot oil—can be dipped in warm soy milk or congee.

Next, it's time to leave for school and work. People travel nearly everywhere by bicycle, crowding city roads in the mornings and evenings. Most bicycles are old—but they are faster than walking, and are affordable for the average person. In cities, motorbikes are becoming a more popular mode of transportation, buzzing up and down the streets and sidewalks.

After school and work, families are reunited by around 6 P.M. and sit down soon after for the evening meal. A Chinese teenager might have the job of fixing dinner for the family. First, a pot of water for cooking rice is put on the stove to boil. If duck with almond is on the menu, fresh duck meat is cut into thin slices and stir-fried in a wok. After a few minutes, peas, mushrooms, and celery slices are added, along with vegetable broth and soy sauce.

In China, grains are the biggest part of every meal. People who live in the north eat mostly wheat products, such as noodles and bread, because wheat

For the majority of people living in rural areas, the bicycle is the most common means of transportation.

Getting Around

Most people in China do not have cars, but both foreign and domestic-made automobiles are becoming increasingly common as people in large cities and suburbs are able to afford them. Cars are still considered a sign of wealth; the average car-owning family has just one.

The minimum age for a driver's license is 18. In mainland China, people drive vehicles on the right side of the road. In Hong Kong, however, people drive vehicles on the left, because this city was once a part of the British Empire.

Buses are a cheap way to travel in the cities, but they are notoriously crowded, with riders standing elbow-to-elbow during busy times. People may have to wait a long time at bus stops, because the buses that arrive are already packed. These buses also produce a lot of exhaust. Because of severe problems with air pollution in its cities, China has begun using hybrid electric buses. These buses reduce exhaust fumes by one-third and reduce noise pollution as well. For those who can afford them, taxis are available but are usually slow because of traffic congestion. The larger cities also have subways or light rail metro train systems, which are a quick and easy way to get around.

The metro train system in Hong Kong has more than six lines and runs through 51 stations.

grows well in the cool, dry weather. In the south, people eat more rice, a crop that thrives in the hot, steamy climate.

Food is purchased daily at canopied outdoor market stalls, where merchants display baskets of colorful fruits and freshly picked vegetables next to tables stacked with raw fish and fresh meat. Shoppers there haggle with merchants to get the best prices possible, then take their purchases home to prepare.

Often, the food is cut into small pieces and stir-fried in a wok with a small amount of oil. This quick cooking method developed in places where fuel was scarce. Other foods, such as dumplings, are steamed rather than stir-fried. Potstickers, or dumplings, are made from thin pastry circles filled with chopped meats and vegetables.

Eggs, chicken, duck, pork, beef, and lamb are common ingredients in

Roast duck is a popular menu item.

Chinese meals. People who live near the ocean also enjoy seafood such as fish, shrimp, squid, clams, and crabs. All kinds of vegetables—cabbage, onion, celery, soybeans, scallions, sweet potatoes, mushrooms, bean sprouts, snow peas, and bamboo shoots—add flavor and nutrition to the traditional Chinese meal.

Food in China is typically served in bowls. Soup broths will be sipped right from the bowl, but chopsticks are the proper utensils for eating any solid foods. The proper way to eat rice in China is to hold the bowl up close to your face and scoop the rice into your mouth with chopsticks.

Although soft drinks and bottled juices are available, China is known for its hot green tea, which is served in small cups and sipped slowly while relaxing and visiting with friends.

Modern Society Woes

Some health problems that result from a poor diet are starting to appear in China. The traditional Chinese diet, which has very little fat or sugar, is extremely healthy. People are also fairly active, often riding bicycles or walking from place to place. In remote villages, children are usually thin. However, fast foods such as fried chicken, cheeseburgers, and french fries are available in cities. These foods have contributed to obesity among some teens—between 7 percent and 11 percent of Chinese teens are overweight. The availability of

A vendor sells fish at a busy street market in Hong Kong.

public transportation and cars in metropolitan areas means that residents are also becoming less active. In addition, many teens relax by watching television or playing computer games, instead of going outdoors to run around.

Other health problems result from air and water pollution. Smog creates significant air pollution in urban areas, such as Liaoning Province in northeast China, where factories use coal for energy and spew unfiltered smoke into the atmosphere. Second-hand smoke is also a serious problem because 67 percent of men and 4 percent of women smoke. Nearly half the people in China are regularly exposed to second-hand smoke. Smoking rates are on the rise among teens in China, as advertising grabs their attention. As a result, respiratory disease and death rates are higher

Chinese Specialties

The Chinese occasionally eat foods such as snake meat, pigeon, eel, shark fin, and soft-shelled turtle. Dog meat also was popular, because it was believed to increase one's circulation. But recently, the number of Chinese dogs that have been registered as pets in urban areas of China has more than tripled, and now people are much less likely to consume them.

A family enjoys a meal at a vegetarian restaurant in Sichuan Province.

為大眾健康著想，會展中心將於
2006年1月1日起全面禁煙。

For your health and comfort,
HKCEC will be a smoke-free venue
effective 1 January 2006.

A sign at the Hong Kong Convention Center announced that the facility would be smoke free in 2006.

in China than in countries with pollution controls and smoking laws.

Fertilizers, pesticides, and untreated industrial waste have polluted the water supply in parts of China. Throughout recent history, Chinese people have had to boil tap water to make it safe to drink. These environmental issues are a concern for many teens, who are old enough to realize how their health may be affected. The Chinese government has recognized these problems and is starting to respond with policies that reduce air and water pollution.

Treatment for pollution-related illness and other conditions is available in major cities at hospitals that offer modern medical care from physicians. In the less-populated areas of China, however, health care is often unavailable or too far away. It's also very expensive, because health insurance is uncommon, so 50 percent to 80 percent of people choose not to go to hospitals because of the cost. Many people—including teens—still prefer traditional Chinese medicine, using acupuncture and herbs to treat minor illnesses.

There are more than 145 million males in China who are under the age of 15, while there are only 128.4 million females in that same age group.

3

Love & Loyalty

WHETHER THEY LIVE in the sparsely populated west or growing cities in the east, and regardless of their lifestyles or livelihoods, the Chinese people share a belief in the importance of family. Love, respect, loyalty, and obligation toward one's family members—living relatives and dead ancestors—are of the utmost importance in Chinese society.

The typical Chinese family consists of just one child who lives with his or her parents and perhaps grandparents. Before the 1970s, it was common to have five or six children in a family. But the population was growing too large for the amount of food the country could produce. In the late 1970s, the Chinese

Until 2004, families with more than one child were fined, sometimes 10 times their yearly income. Now the Chinese government rewards people who have followed the rules, rather than punishing those who have not.

government created laws to limit the number of children in each family. Now parents in most cities have only one child. In rural areas, people may have two children if their first baby is a girl, and in some isolated ethnic groups, two or three children are allowed. These laws have had the effect of slowing down the population growth.

Today most teens in China are growing up as only children, and this is what seems normal to them. Because

Chinese families are now so small, most teens are treasured and indulged by their parents. Those who act spoiled are called "Little Emperors."

In China, many couples feel that it's very important to have a son. Historically, sons were considered vital in Chinese society because they carry on the family name—an important link to the ancestors of the past. Family lineage, which shows how people are related through the generations, is traced only through sons. Some people can trace their family lineage back 2,500 years! People also want sons because they think boys contribute greater physical labor to a family. In a society that is mostly agricultural, this is of great importance. Millions of small family farmers still do work by hand, because modern machinery is not available or affordable. In some places, the

Farmers harvesting rice from terraced fields still do so by hand.

land is so steep or rocky that machines can't be used. Parents need the help a strong son can provide.

In addition, sons are expected to support and care for their parents as they grow old. Because family bonds are very important in China, most teens want and expect to eventually take care of their parents.

Some Chinese parents give up their baby girls because they desperately want to try and have baby boys. Sometimes foreigners or humanitarian organizations adopt these abandoned baby girls. Because of this, an imbalance has developed in China's population. Instead of nearly equal numbers of boys and girls, now there are about 113 boys for every 100 girls in China. When

these Chinese boys grow up and want to have families of their own, some will not be able to find wives. The Chinese government estimates that by 2020, there could be as many as 25 million bachelors in China.

When Chinese children do grow up and marry, tradition dictates that a daughter will leave home to live with her husband's family. A son brings his new wife home to live with his family—as his father did before him—and he eventually inherits the family home. This is still true for most people who live in rural China, but traditions are changing in the cities. Now after marriage, couples in cities sometimes live in buildings with groups of co-workers rather than with the husband's parents.

In farming communities, newborn girls are considered to be unlucky, and this belief has led to the abandonment of baby girls.

Some employers have everything on site, including dormitories and small hospitals for employees.

After couples have children, the husband's parents often move in with their son's family to help care for the grandchildren. This benefits young parents, who often work long hours. Most teens expect their parents to help them in this way when they have children.

Confucianism, a philosophy practiced in China since about 500 B.C., stresses strong respect for elders. Children are taught that every family member should contribute to the family's welfare and that they should behave honorably to avoid bringing shame onto the family. As a result, each child's success or failure in life reflects on the family.

Today the success of the individual has become more important than ever before. Many teens are very focused on their future careers and hope to become successful and rich.

Confucius

The Communist Party in China declares the country to be officially atheist, but many people throughout the country practice some sort of religion, including Confucianism, Daoism, Buddhism, Islam, and Christianity.

Perhaps the most influential philosopher in China, Confucius' (551-479 B.C.) teachings have influenced social behavior in China for more than 2,000 years. Confucius stressed filial piety, or family loyalty to those living and dead. He emphasized honesty, moral behavior, and respect for elders or those in higher positions. He thought each person should perform his or her role in society in a responsible way. Confucius also advised people to follow what some people now call the Golden Rule: "Do not do to others what you do not want them to do to you."

Confucianism is an important part of China's culture. Chinese teens are expected to love and respect their parents, be courteous and considerate, and maintain peaceful relationships with others. Another teaching is particularly useful to young scholars: "I hear and I forget. I see and I remember. I do and I understand."

The Good Life

Teenagers in China cite internationally-known, successful sports figures as their role models— such as basketball stars Yao Ming, Michael Jordan, and Kobe Bryant, and soccer star David Beckham. They also look up to executives such as Kai-Fu Lee, head of Google operations in China and Bill Gates, head of Microsoft Corporation. Many Chinese teens want to have prestigious jobs, large homes, and lots of money to spend when they grow up. Even teens who live in rural areas are aware of this kind of lifestyle and wish for better opportunities than they might have expected before television and the Internet linked them to the rest of the world.

One of the signs of modern life is a cell phone. Cell phones are widely used to stay in touch, especially in populated areas of China. In rural areas, some people have no phone service of any kind, but development is not far off. Efforts are being made to modernize the remote areas of western China.

China's Superstar Athletes

Li Ning

This former gymnast won six gold medals at the 1984 Summer Olympics in Los Angeles. In 1990, he founded the Beijing Li-Ning Sports Goods Company. His company's revenues In 2005 exceeded 2,359,650,000 yuan (U.S.$300 million).

Liu Xiang

This hurdling superstar won a gold medal in the 110-meter hurdles event at the 2004 Summer Olympics. In 2006, he broke the world record in the 110-meter hurdles.

Fu Mingxia

At just 13 years old, she became the youngest Olympic champion ever, when she won the gold medal for the 10-meter platform diving event in 1992. Among her other achievements, she also won the gold medal in the 3-meter springboard event at the 2000 Olympic Games.

Yao Ming, a 7-foot, 6-inch (228.6-centimeter) center, started his career in Chinese basketball at just 17 years old. In 2002, he signed with the U.S. NBA team, the Houston Rockets.

43

In 2004, nearly 335 million cell phones were in use across China, in addition to 263 million landlines.

Friends & Activities

As in other countries, Chinese kids meet most of their friends at school or during activities such as Young Pioneers, or the Communist Youth League, communist organizations for children and teens. Team sports such as soccer, basketball, swimming, and gymnastics are very popular among young people, as are table tennis and bowling. Video and computer games, such as *World of Warcraft*, are exceedingly popular in China. Teens play on home computers or go with friends to Internet cafes, which provide as many as 120 terminals per location for games, research, or online chats. Parties are not common, but many teens go out to dance or sing karaoke. In the cities, people can also go to movies, concerts, and professional sporting events. In the country, teens gather at local festivals to meet people and to participate in activities.

Typically, teens do not start dating until after high school. Before the current generation, parents were responsible for finding suitable partners for their children. Sometimes a bride and groom did not even meet until their wedding day. Today people usually choose their own spouses. In most of China, men must be at least 22 and women at least 20 years old to marry, but the government encourages them to wait until they are even older. Young people now marry for love, but they usually also seek partners of good moral character who can offer financial security.

Chinese Names

Chinese names begin with the surname (family name), followed by the individual's given name—the opposite of Western countries, which use the given (first) name before the family name. If your name were John Smith in a Western country, in China you would be known as Smith John. The family name is considered the most important in China, because a person is defined by the family. For that reason, women do not change their names when they get married. Family names are passed down from the father to the children.

Typically, the family name has just one syllable, and the given name has

A single woman participating in a dating service game holds a heart that symbolizes love. Some busy young people choose to use dating services to meet others.

two. In China, the top three Chinese surnames are: Zhang, Wang, and Li. In fact, 100 million people have the name Zhang. In China, there are only about 300 commonly used surnames, compared to English-speaking countries, in which there are thousands. On the other hand, there is much more variety in given names among the Chinese than among English-speaking people.

Within families people are addressed by their roles—such as Mother, Father, Older Sister, or Uncle— rather than by their names. The Chinese

The gender and placement of each family member are understood in a single Chinese word.

language has many more words to describe family members than do most Western languages. For example, in English, a cousin is simply the child of an aunt or uncle. In Chinese, a single word indicates whether the cousin is a male or female from the mother's or the father's side of the family. The same holds true for the word *uncle*: In China, the word chosen indicates whether the uncle is an older or younger brother of the mother or father. In China, *bobo* refers to the father's older brother, *shushu* is the father's younger brother; and *jiujiu* is the word used for the mother's brother.

Nicknames are commonly used for close friends or relatives. Lao, which means old, and Xiao, which means young, are frequently used. A teen with the surname Zhang might be called Zhang Xiao, while his father or grandfather might be called Zhang Lao. Other nicknames are based on where a person is born, a physical characteristic, or an accomplishment. Many Chinese teens adopt English nicknames once they start learning English in school. Often they choose names they hear on television, such as those of sports stars or television characters.

bobo
BWO-bwo
shushu
SHOO-shoo
jiujiu
JOE-joe

What's In a Name
Popular Chinese Names

Male Names

Name	Meaning
De	virtue, virtuous
Wen	culture, cultured
Yong	courage, courageous

Female Names

Name	Meaning
Lian	lotus
Min	clever, witty
Ying	brave, beautiful

Male or Female Names

Name	Meaning
Chun	springtime
Ming	bright, clear
Xiao	dawn

Folk dancers carry lanterns through the streets of Beijing as part of the Chinese New Year celebration.

4 Red is for Luck

ALTHOUGH WORK IS IMPORTANT, so are holidays in China. The country has many national and traditional holidays. Chinese teens join their families in celebrating the Chinese New Year and the Mid-Autumn Festival—the most significant of the traditional Chinese holidays—as well as some new holidays, such as Christmas. Weddings, births, and funerals are other occasions that bring families together.

The most important holiday in China is the Chinese New Year, also known as the Spring Festival. The Chinese New Year celebrates the first day of the lunar calendar, which begins with the first new moon of the year. The date varies between late January and mid-February each year. This holiday has

National Holidays Calendar

Official National Holidays

New Year's Day—January 1
Spring Festival or Lunar New Year—January or February
Labor Day—May 1
National Day—October 1

Other Celebrations

International Working Women's Day—March 8
Tree Planting Day—March 12
Pure Brightness Day—April 5
Youth Day—May 4
International Children's Day—June 1
Chinese Communist Party Founding Day—July 1
People's Liberation Army Founding Day—August 1
Double Ninth Festival—September
Teachers' Day—September 10

been celebrated in China for more than 4,000 years. Since 1999, citizens have received an entire week off from work and school, and this is known as one of three Golden Weeks in China.

The Spring Festival lasts for 15 days, but preparations begin a month beforehand. People clean their houses from top to bottom so they can sweep away bad luck. They paint their doorways red and decorate them with paper scrolls bearing blessings and wishes for happiness, good fortune, wealth, and long life. Potted plants—especially those in bloom—decorate homes to signify new life and prosperity. In order to have a fresh start for the coming year, people get haircuts, buy new clothes, and pay off old debts.

On New Year's Eve, family members travel long distances so they can be together for the holiday. A large meal is prepared using special foods that symbolize good wishes for the coming year. For example, an entire chicken might be served complete with its head, tail, and feet to symbolize prosperity. A whole fish represents togetherness. Dumplings shaped like ancient Chinese

Entertainers perform a lion dance on the eve of the Chinese New Year.

gold pieces signify wealth. Long, uncut noodles represent long life. *Shengcai*, or lettuce, symbolizes prosperity because the Chinese word sounds like *cai*, the word that means "to bring about wealth and riches." The words for tangerines, oranges, and pomelos sound like the words for "luck," "wealth," and "abundance," respectively, so

shengcai
SHUNG-SAHY

cai
SAHY

51

these are also part of the menu.

After the feast, the entire family stays up until midnight or later, talking about old times and watching holiday specials on TV. Indoor lights remain on for the entire night to welcome in the New Year. In the past, people lit firecrackers at midnight to drive away evil spirits, but this tradition has been outlawed in many cities because of injuries, noise, and pollution. The next morning, on New Year's Day, children receive red packets or envelopes containing "good luck" money from parents, grandparents, and other relatives. Dressed in their new clothes, people visit their friends and neighbors, offering them gifts of food and flowers, and wishing them a happy new year.

After that, things are quiet until the

A family in Shanxi Province in central China enjoy their New Year's Eve meal.

15th day of the New Year, when the first full moon appears, and families gather again. On this day, people eat sticky rice rolled into balls around a sweet filling, the round shape symbolizing wholeness and togetherness. In the evening, it is time for the Lantern Festival. People carrying paper lanterns gather in the streets in a colorful parade. Groups of young men carry enormous figures made of bamboo, paper, and silk for the Lion Dance and Dragon Dance.

The second most important traditional holiday in China is the Mid-Autumn Festival, during which people celebrate the end of the fall harvest. This festival occurs during September or October at the time of the fall equinox, when the moon is full, bright, and very large in the sky. Like the Spring Festival, the Mid-Autumn Festival is a time for family reunions.

According to legend, it also commemorates the victory of the Chinese Ming dynasty over the Yuan dynasty established by Mongol invaders. In 1353, a Ming general had battle plans secretly baked into the bottoms of the cakes served at the Mid-Autumn Festival. He was able to spread the message to friends and relatives, who joined him to overthrow the Mongols.

Because of this legend, moon cakes are the traditional food for the Mid-Autumn Festival. Sweet moon cakes, made from ground lotus seeds and sesame seeds wrapped in flaky pastry, are eaten with pomelos and other

The Chinese Lunar Calendar

The Chinese lunar calendar uses one of 12 different animals to represent each year, in the following order: Rat, Ox, Tiger, Rabbit, Dragon, Snake, Horse, Sheep, Monkey, Chicken, Dog, and Pig. Each animal represents something different. For example, those who are born in the Year of the Dog are said to be loyal, honest, generous, and able to keep secrets. But they are also stubborn, selfish, and aloof, and often find fault with other people. People born in the Year of the Dog are said to be compatible with those born in the Year of the Horse or the Year of the Tiger, but will not get along with those born in the Year of the Dragon.

Moon cakes are traditionally served at a Mid-Autumn Festival meal.

fruits. In the evening, families go to parks and hilltops to enjoy the autumn air and gaze at the moon. Children run around with colorful lanterns while young couples sit together on park benches. Traditionally, those who cannot be with their families on that night look at the moon and think of home. Even though they may be apart, they share the same moon.

Pure Brightness Day, in early April, is a day when people visit the tombs of ancestors and national heroes to pay respects. Families often go out to parks to fly kites and enjoy the warmth of early spring.

The Double Ninth Festival, which takes place on the ninth day of the ninth lunar month, is celebrated with chrysanthemum flowers, in bloom at this time of year. In addition, it is a day to honor the elderly. Teens send presents to their grandparents or other older relatives, and go with them to special programs

A boy prays before he places a candle on a river to mark the Mid-Autumn Festival.

and concerts.

International Labor Day falls on May 1, and citizens receive the following week off from school and work. This week is the second of three Golden Weeks in China. During this time, many families take trips. They might visit tourist attractions such as the Great Wall of

China or Tian'anmen Square in Beijing, or they might take a relaxing vacation in Thailand or Singapore. The trips may vary, but millions of Chinese citizens take advantage of this time to travel.

The third Golden Week begins on October 1, on National Day, which celebrates the anniversary of the founding of the People's Republic of China. Much like the Golden Week of International Labor Day, this week marks another popular time for Chinese citizens to travel.

New Celebrations

Some Chinese are concerned that teens and young adults are losing interest in the traditional festivals and celebrations. Lifestyles are changing, and teens now are less familiar with the old tradtions. People who live in the city do not harvest crops or grow flowers, and often do not find the festivals very meaningful. Instead, many teens are participating in Western holiday celebrations such as Valentine's Day and Christmas.

Young people in Beijing, Shanghai, and Hong Kong embrace Valentine's Day with cards, flowers, and chocolates, but this celebration is still uncommon among older people and in rural communities. Among those groups, in which arranged marriages were common, people have not necessarily married for love.

Christmas, the Christian religious celebration to honor the birth of Jesus, has become a popular new holiday for the Chinese. For many years, it was only celebrated by a small number of Chinese Christians. During the past decade, the Chinese have become familiar with Christmas celebrations

Thousands of people visit Tian'anmen Square in Beijing during the Golden Week of Labor Day.

around the world. Now holiday displays of Christmas trees, lights, and Santa Claus decorate cities all around China. Even non-Christian Chinese have eagerly adopted this holiday as a time for feasting, shopping, giving presents, and visiting friends and family.

Other Celebrations

There are other reasons for celebrations, of course, besides holidays. People everywhere celebrate weddings and engagements. In China, for many centuries, parents arranged weddings for their children. A matchmaker carried a proposal from the boy's parents to the girl's parents. The matchmaker would compare the girl's date and time of birth to astrological signs to determine whether she and the boy were compatible. If they were considered to be compatible, and the two sets of parents agreed, the engagement would take place. A fortune-teller would select the best wedding date based on the birth dates of the bride and groom.

Today young men and women choose their own spouses. Once engaged, the families of the bride and groom exchange gifts. The groom's parents send sweet cakes and tea to the bride's home, and the bride shares them with relatives as she announces her wedding plans. The bride's parents send

Western-style Christmas lights are displayed on a street in Nanjing.

food and sometimes clothing to the groom's family.

Traditionally, when the wedding day arrived, the bride wore a red silk dress—the traditional color for happiness and prosperity—but today many brides also wear a modern, Western white gown. In fact, it is not uncommon for a bride to wear several dresses for the wedding day. Usually the bride wears a white dress for the ceremony, a traditional red dress for the banquet, and another dress to leave the banquet. Only immediate family members attend the wedding. After the wedding, a ban-

quet for friends and family celebrates the happy occasion.

The birth of a baby is also a time for joy. New mothers spend a month at home, relaxing and caring for the baby. After a month, family and friends attend a celebration that welcomes the new child. The child's parents give gifts of red eggs, which symbolize happiness and harmony, to relatives and friends. In return, visitors often give gifts of money wrapped in red paper.

Babies are considered 1 year old at birth. And no matter when they were actually born, everyone is counted a

A couple traditionally wears red on their wedding day.

RED IS FOR LUCK

A family in Hong Kong burns funeral money, offering it to the deceased.

year older at the Chinese New Year. Traditionally, people didn't celebrate birthdays until they turn 60. After that, they celebrated every 10 years, at age 70 and 80 and so on. Long, uncut noodles might be served at those birthday celebrations to symbolize long life. Today birthdays have become popular celebrations for family members and close friends, at any age.

When someone dies, the family gathers for the funeral. Loud wailing and crying demonstrate respect for an older person who has died. If a young person has died, however, the mourners will be silent, because the Chinese do not typically believe in showing respect to someone who is younger

than oneself. People dress according to their relationship with the person who has died. The immediate family wears black. Grandchildren wear blue clothes, and great-grandchildren wear light blue. Burials take place at cemeteries that are located on hillsides according to the principles of *feng shui,* a method of arranging places occupied by people to ensure harmony with nature. The Chinese believe that seven days after a person has died, their soul returns to their home.

feng shui
FUNG SHWAY

The Chinese government does not set a national minimum wage. Each province sets its own minimum wage standard.

5

Teens at Work

IN CHINA, MOST TEENS EVENTUALLY CHOOSE TO WORK in the same career as their parents. Because China has relatively few colleges and universities compared to the huge number of applicants, senior middle school students usually begin jobs after graduation at age 18. Some teens begin working when they are younger, after finishing junior middle school, because they need to earn money to support themselves or their families.

If work is not available, or money is scarce, many young people leave their families to join the crowds of migrants in China. About 80 percent of this "floating population" is between the ages of 15 and 35 years old. Usually, they move from rural to urban areas, from the less-

61

Crops & Industry

The type of work a Chinese person performs varies depending on where he or she lives. The majority of people still work in agriculture. China is such a large country that it spans several climate zones, ranging from subarctic in the northwest to tropical in the southeast.

To the north is Inner Mongolia, a region of mountains, plateaus, deserts, and vast grasslands that feed herds of domestic animals. In this area, the winters are long and cold, with frequent blizzards, while summers are short, but hot. The main crops are wheat, corn, millet, and cotton. Miners excavate large coal and mineral deposits in this part of China.

The central region, in the Yangtze River Basin, is known as the "rice bowl" of China. This is the richest agricultural area of the country. Here the soil is fertile, rain is plentiful, and temperatures are mild enough to grow crops all year long. Irrigated rice paddies in the basin produce more rice than any other place in the world. Sweet potatoes, peanuts, and sesame are also grown here.

In southern China, the climate is tropical, with abundant rain and a long growing season, but the terrain is so hilly that it is difficult to grow crops. Here the main crops are rice, sugarcane, mulberries, and fruit. Pigs, ducks, chickens, and geese are raised here in large numbers. Fish farms, or fisheries, are located in ponds and in the shallow coastal areas, where fresh and marine fish are grown and harvested.

China has the world's largest fishing industry, with one-third of the world's total production. The Yellow Sea and the East China Sea are shallow bodies of water, and fish farms there produce most of the catch. Because of over fishing in the coastal areas, Chinese officials have promoted the use of marine and freshwater fish farms (aquaculture), and in 2003, they reduced the number of fishing boats by 30,000.

Terraced rice paddies are a common site along the Yangtze River Basin.

developed areas in the west to more developed areas in the east. Moves across province boundaries are officially prohibited, and until recently, millions of migrants were not counted when the government calculated the populations of Chinese cities. Yet the migrants provide the manual labor needed for factories, the service industries, and the huge construction projects taking place in the cities. Because migrants are unofficial workers, they often have trouble collecting their wages, and their living conditions are poor. Nearly 20 million of the 100 million migrants in China are children.

The average worker in China earns less than 7,866 yuan (U.S.$1,005) per year, but income varies widely. While

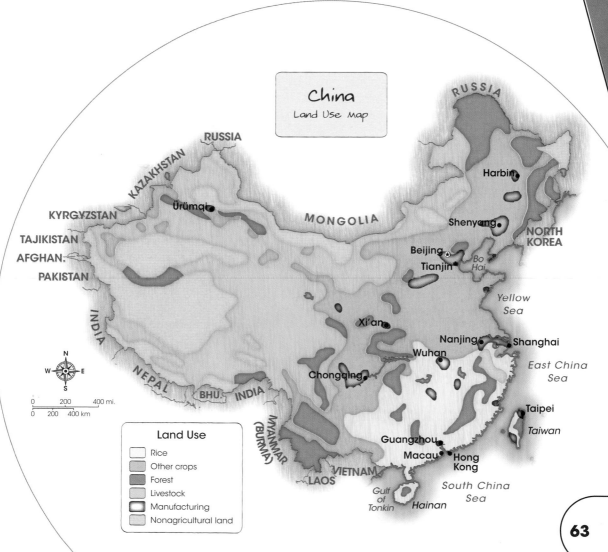

China
Land Use Map

RUSSIA

KAZAKHSTAN

RUSSIA

Ürümqi

MONGOLIA

Harbin

Shenyang

NORTH KOREA

KYRGYZSTAN

TAJIKISTAN

AFGHAN.

PAKISTAN

Beijing

Tianjin

Bo Hai

Yellow Sea

INDIA

NEPAL

BHU.

INDIA

MYANMAR (BURMA)

Xi'an

Nanjing

Shanghai

Wuhan

Chongqing

East China Sea

Taipei

Taiwan

N W E S

0   200   400 mi.
0   200   400 km

Guangzhou

Macau   Hong Kong

VIETNAM

LAOS

Gulf of Tonkin

Hainan

South China Sea

Land Use

- ☐ Rice
- ☐ Other crops
- ☐ Forest
- ☐ Livestock
- ☐ Manufacturing
- ☐ Nonagricultural land

the average Shanghai resident earns nearly 39,328 yuan (U.S.$5,024) per year, a worker in rural China earns less than 3,146 yuan (U.S.$402) per year. More than 80 million peasants earn less than 787 yuan (U.S.$101) per year, the official poverty level in China. Unemployment is about 9 percent in cities but is as high as 20 percent overall. People who have attended vocational-technical schools have more opportunities available to them. The best-paid workers are college graduates.

Even those who go to college may have trouble finding jobs when they graduate. According to the Personnel Ministry of China, in 2003 there were approximately 5.1 million people looking for jobs (2.7 million of whom were college graduates), but only 2.4 million jobs were available. Because of the extreme competition, entry-level salaries in many cities were one-third less in 2005 than the year before. In Beijing, for example, monthly salaries dropped from 2,000 to 3,000 yuan (U.S.$255 to $383) to 1,000 to 2,000 yuan (U.S.$127 to $255). In Chengdu, 700 to 800 yuan (U.S.$89 to $102) per month has become the norm. Some new graduates fear they will not earn enough to pay back their parents or their student loans.

Some of the top jobs for new graduates in 2005 were in sales and marketing, engineering, and computer science. More jobs are available to those who are fluent in both Chinese and English. However, many new jobs are becoming available in small cities in central and western China, as companies in the large eastern cities seek to expand their business to the rest of the country. Those students who continue beyond college to attend graduate school, especially in the sciences, still face competition. But the Chinese government and foreign investors are expanding

Division of Labor in China

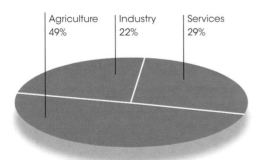

Agriculture 49%

Industry 22%

Services 29%

Source: United States Central Intelligence Agency.
The World Factbook—China.

In 2007, 4.13 million students are expected to graduate from college, but only 1.66 million of them will find jobs.

the number and quality of scientific research labs throughout the country. They hope to keep graduates from leaving the country, and also hope to lure back Chinese students who have gone to foreign universities.

Whether they are students or not, all male and female teens must register for military service when they turn 18.

From the ages of 18 to 22, teens may be called up to serve for two years if needed. In addition, those who have already served on active duty may be called back into the military if needed. Most military officers are graduates of military academies or universities.

According to the China's constitution, "It is the sacred obligation of every citizen

At Central South University, students work at the national laboratory for medical genetics.

of the People's Republic of China to defend the motherland and resist aggression. It is the honorable duty of citizens of the People's Republic of China to perform military service and join the militia in accordance with the law."

Most teens have been taught the importance of serving their country and understand that they might have to serve.

The People's Liberation Army (PLA) is the largest branch of the Chinese military and includes the ground forces, navy, air force, and artillery corps (strategic missile force). The other branches are the armed police force—which provides security guards, defense for borders, fire teams, and other local security—and the militia, groups of men and women between 18 and 35 who can provide local assistance to the military if needed. In 2005, China had approximately 300 million people available for military duty.

People who have served in the military are usually offered govern-

Students take part in military training through their university studies. They are credited for their performance.

ment jobs, such as city or provincial administrators. Many people compete for these types of civil service positions, which offer regular hours, job security, and sometimes even free or low-cost housing. In China, the Communist Party of China (CPC) is in charge of the country at both the national and local levels. Only people who are members of the CPC may serve in government or political jobs. Chinese citizens who are at least 18 years old may apply for membership in the CPC if they accept and support party principles and are willing to participate and pay dues. The national government selects the people who may run for office, and voters, who are age 18 and up, choose among those candidates in local elections. Many teens join the CPC as a way to broaden their job opportunities.

Teens skateboard in
the People's Square
in Shanghai.

6

Having Fun in a Country of Change

wequi
way-CHEE

IT'S SATURDAY and in the southeastern city of Guangzhou teens are playing in the park. One group kicks a soccer ball from player to player; another group practices tae kwon do. Kites drift overhead in the light breeze. At the school, the drama club practices for an upcoming play, and the science club prepares for a contest.

Traditional activities such as painting, calligraphy, music, Chinese opera, and the game of wequi have entertained Chinese people for thousands of years. Today sports, television, rock music, and travel offer modern entertainment as well.

Team sports such as volleyball, basketball, and soccer are common after school activities. Bowling, golf, and tennis are also on the rise. Teens in China say they like trying new activities that are

69

different from what their parents enjoy. Outdoor activities such as rock climbing, hiking, skiing, and snowboarding are new to the Chinese, but these sports are catching on quickly, especially among young people.

For those who can afford to travel, the mountains of central and western China offer scenic playgrounds. In northeast China, ski resorts have been built in the hilly terrain around Beijing, which has winter temperatures ranging from 15 to 40 degrees Fahrenheit (9 below to 4 degrees Celsius). Because Beijing gets very little winter precipitation, snow machines are used to keep the slopes covered. However, man-made snow production has been threatened

Yabuli is one of China's premier ski resorts, boasting an average of 170 days of snow per year.

HAVING FUN IN A
COUNTRY OF CHANGE

by water shortages in recent years.

China was named host of the 2008 Summer Olympics in Beijing. Since 1984, Chinese athletes have participated in the Olympic Games, winning medals in table tennis, badminton, diving, swimming, volleyball, gymnastics, and skating, among others.

The Chinese government sponsors the training of thousands of young athletes at specialty schools. Training officials visit elementary schools to observe children's physical education classes, and they select promising athletes who are just 6 or 7 years old. These children are sent to athletic training schools—sometimes far from home—where they work for hours every day to perfect their skills in the sport that is chosen for them. Many of these athletes will train hard but will never participate in international competitions, because only the very best are selected.

Basketball player Yao Ming, of the Houston Rockets, is a hero to Chinese teens, who eagerly follow his career in the United States. The son of two Chinese basketball stars, Yao attended an athletic training school as a child. He began his career in the Chinese Basketball Association, playing for the Shanghai Sharks. He gained international recognition for his performance on the court, and the Rockets recruited him in 2002.

Many Chinese teens watch sports on television, but other shows also draw their attention. China Central Television

The 2008 Beijing Olympics logo is called "Dancing Beijing" and was designed by Guo Chunning.

(CCTV), a government-controlled television network, offers national news, sports, music, movies, children's shows, educational programs, and documentaries. Regional and city television channels provide local news coverage and information. Digital programming is available in many cities across China.

Soap opera dramas are by far the most popular shows in China. A South Korean soap opera, *Dae Jang Geum* (*Jewel in the Palace*) tells the story of the first female physician in the Korean royal palace, and it has drawn record numbers of viewers.

Reality shows have also taken hold. In the show *Women in Control*, men compete in intellectual, physical, and talent contests, while female audience members choose the winner. On *TV Court*, family court disputes are re-enacted for television. *Super Girl*, a singing contest, captured the attention of television audiences across China in 2005. And Chinese teens have become familiar with the animated series *Sponge Bob Square Pants* and *The Wild Thornberrys*.

Music is an important part of the lives of most teenagers, and Chinese teens are no exception. At the 12th Chinese Music Awards in 2006, 27-year-old singer-songwriter Jay Chow of Taiwan was the big winner. Frequently mentioned as a favorite in music blogs, Chow composes and performs pop, rock, rap, and rhythm and blues. Other popular Chinese singers include female artists Jolin Tsai and Fish Leong, and bands Yu Quan, F.I.R., Flowers, and Twins.

Members of the studio audience show a poster of the winner of the television show *Super Girl*.

Since computers have become widely available, urban teens who don't have access to a computer at home can visit Internet cafes in order to play games, search for information, or communicate with others via e-mail or in chat rooms. Internet service providers (ISPs) must be careful to limit what is available, however. The Chinese government prohibits any information or activities that might undermine its authority or promote dissatisfaction or protests among the people. Sites that include significant religious, sexual, or violent content are also prohibited. ISPs that allow illegal Web sites face punishment, and government officials often monitors users' viewing habits and e-mail transmissions. This means that Chinese citizens only have access to what the communist government allows, although some people are able to find ways around the government blockades.

Most cities have movie theaters that remain busy, even though the price—20 yuan (U.S.$2.56) on average,

Cui Jian

The most famous rock musician in China is 45-year-old Cui Jian, considered the "Father of Chinese rock." A trumpet player as a teen, he performed with the Beijing Philharmonic Orchestra. After hearing tapes of the Beatles, the Rolling Stones, John Denver, and singers Simon and Garfunkel, he was inspired to learn guitar and form his own rock band. Since 1985, he has continued to explore musical styles such as folk music, jazz, and punk rock, and has performed at concert halls worldwide.

and as much as 80 yuan (U.S.$10.22) in large cities—is very high for most Chinese workers.

China still allows only 20 foreign films into the country each year, and some must be edited to meet government standards. For example, movies are rejected by a regulatory board if they include anything that might be offensive to the Chinese people, but the board is not clear as to what "offensive" means. China's own film industry, however, is growing quickly and now ranks third worldwide, after the U.S. and Indian film industries. Favorite actors Jet Li, Chow Yun-Fat, Jackie Chan, Michelle Yeoh, Gong Li, and Ziyi Zhang are well known in China and internationally. Recent films produced in China include *House of Flying Daggers*, *Hero*, and *The Road Home*.

Seeing the Sights

For many people, the perfect way to relax is to take a trip. There are many places to visit in China, and increasingly, the Chinese can afford to travel. Modern expressways span the country. Paved and well marked, these roads have speed limits of 62 to 74 miles (99 to 118 km) per hour. Signs provide information in Chinese and English. Buses and trucks are the main form of transportation on the expressways. The National Trunk Highway System is still under construction but is expected to be completed in 2020. Most highways are still rough and unpaved.

Trains are the best way to go from city to city. Some trains connect to adjacent countries like Russia, Mongolia,

The National Trunk Highway System already includes more than 25,000 miles (41,000 km) of expressways.

Vietnam, and North Korea. Passenger trains, some with sleeper cars, allow people to quickly travel long distances.

Perhaps the most famous place for Chinese tourists to visit is the Great Wall of China. This 4,000-mile (6,400-km) brick and stone wall stretches east to west across northern China. The Great Wall as we know it today was completed during the Ming dynasty to defend China against Mongolian and Turkish invaders from the north. The original wall took 10 years and thousands of workers to complete. Later rulers added to the wall during the centuries that followed.

The Forbidden City in Beijing

The Great Wall of China is composed of many walls that are connected and were built throughout numerous dynasties.

Trains

New high-speed trains run at speeds of 124 to 186 miles (198 to 298 km) per hour between several large cities. The world's first magnetic levitation train operates out of Shanghai. Also known as a maglev train, it uses opposing magnets to levitate the train over a guide track. It has reached speeds as high as 267 miles (427 km) per hour. The Qinghai-Tibet railway is the newest of China's rail lines. It stretches 710 miles (1,136 km) from northwest to southwest China, from Qinghai Province to Tibet. It travels across the Tibetan Plateau through one of the most mountainous regions in the world. Nearly 600 miles (960 km) of track are higher than 13,000 feet (3,965 meters); the highest point travels through the Tanggula Mountain Pass, at 16,640 feet (5,075 m). Trains that run on these tracks have pressurized cabins, since there is so little oxygen in the air at such high altitudes.

Shanghai's maglev train arrives at Long Yang Station after its trip from Pudong airport in Shanghai.

HAVING FUN IN A COUNTRY OF CHANGE

was the Imperial Palace for 24 emperors of the Ming dynasty and Qing dynasty. Called the Forbidden City because there were some areas where only the emperor and his family were allowed to go, its 900 symmetrically arranged buildings are surrounded by 30-foot (9-meter) walls and a 20-foot (6-meter) moat. Today it is known as the Palace Museum and is one of the most visited monuments in China. Tian'anmen Square, named for the Gate of Heavenly Peace that provides access to the Forbidden City, is located across the street.

Xian was the ancient capital city for 11 dynasties. In 1974, a farmer digging a well discovered the enormous tomb of China's first emperor, Qin Shihuang (259–210 B.C.). Protecting

The Forbidden City is located in the center of Beijing and was built during the Ming dynasty (1368–1644).

the emperor's tomb were thousands of life-size men and horses made of terra-cotta, arranged in military formation. The warriors were sculpted in intricate detail, each wearing individual uniforms and bearing facial expressions. More than 7,000 warriors, horses, weapons, and other pieces have been unearthed. The tomb and these magnificent warriors are on public display at The Museum of Terra Cotta Warriors and

Horses, and archeologists continue to excavate the site.

Shanghai is the biggest city in China and is known for its cosmopolitan flair. Many of the wealthiest Chinese live and work in Shanghai, and there is a greater focus on fashion and fine living than in other parts of China. The city has an abundance of cultural, sporting, shopping, and entertainment opportunities. Teens here are likely to spend their

The terra-cotta warriors were each buried with a weapon, such as a spear. It is believed that the weapons were used in actual combat.

free time at clubs or the cinema, or shopping for the latest fashions or electronics.

One hour west of Shanghai, the small city of Suzhou lures visitors with its scenic gardens, canals, and stone bridges. A Chinese proverb says, "In heaven there is paradise, on earth Hangzhou and Suzhou." The city is also famous for its role in the silk industry. The silk produced in Suzhou was made into clothing for emperors and was traded to foreign merchants by way of the ancient Silk Road. The Suzhou Silk Museum and several silk factories offer demonstrations of this ancient technique.

The Three Gorges of the Yangtze River provides some of the most spectacular scenery in the country. The river winds between steep rocky cliffs that reach as high as 3,000 feet (915 m) above the water. For now, tourists can take river cruises to explore these canyons, but not for much longer. The canyons

The Three Gorges is a popular spot for Chinese tourists to visit.

Nanjing Road is the main shopping area in Shanghai. Its western end is known for its luxurious shopping centers.

are to be filled by a 400-mile (640-km) reservoir after the completion of the Three Gorges Dam. In Wuhan, a city of 7 million at the confluence of the Yangtze and Han rivers, teens can enjoy swimming or boating at beautiful East Lake. The canyon gorges of nearby Qingjiang River, a branch of the Yangtze, offer white-water rafting to adventurous visitors.

These well-known attractions traditionally draw many visitors, but Chinese youth are starting their own traditions. Hiking and camping are activities that were relatively unknown in China until several years ago, but both are gaining in popularity among teens and young adults. Youth hostels, located in cities across the nation, provide inexpensive, no-frills lodging for young tourists.

The Yangtze River

The Yangtze River, at more than 3,964 miles (6,342 km), is the third longest river in the world, after the Nile River in Egypt and the Amazon River in Brazil. Boats use the Yangtze to move goods between central China and the coast at Shanghai, where the river empties into the East China Sea.

A huge project is under way to build the Three Gorges Dam across the Yangtze River. By far the largest in the world, this 1½-mile (2.4-km) dam is designed to prevent the devastating floods that have killed a million people in the last 100 years. A series of locks will allow ocean-going ships to go 1,500 miles (2,400 km) upriver to the city of Chongqing.

The dam will turn the Yangtze into a power source that generates huge amounts of electricity, helping to combat the severe air pollution that now plagues China. But it will also create a reservoir that will submerge parts of the breathtaking Three Gorges canyons and more than 100 towns along the river.

Looking Ahead

TEENS IN CHINA TODAY have many more opportunities than their parents and grandparents did, and they are optimistic about their futures.

Although China is a place where some activities are restricted by government regulations, Chinese citizens are seeing fewer rules than ever before. Literacy and education are at an all-time high, and information from foreign places is shaping the way the Chinese view their future. Teens, especially, want to have it all: high-paying jobs, roomy homes, fashionable clothing, automobiles, and a chance to see the world. They also want choices—something their parents did not often experience—in spouses, employers, and leisure activities.

Chinese teens are bound by tradition as well. They feel a natural, cultural obligation to obey, remain close to, and eventually help take care of their parents. While old traditions are being preserved, new ones are being added, and all of these traditions define a Chinese teen's identity.

At a Glance

Official name: People's Republic of China

Capital: Beijing

People

Population: 1,306,313,812

Population by age group:

0–14 years: 21.4%
15–64 years: 71%
65 years and up: 7.6%

Life expectancy at birth: 72.27 years

Official language: Mandarin Chinese

Other common languages: Cantonese, Shanghaiese, Fuzhou, Hokkien-Taiwanese, Xiang, Gan

Religion:

Buddhist: 20–25%
Christian: 3–4%
Daoist (Taoist): unknown
Muslim: 1–2%
Note: China is officially atheist

Legal ages:

Driver's license: 18
Marriage: Men 22; women 20
Military service: 18–22 for compulsory service
Voting: 18

Government

Type of government: Communist

Chief of state: President

Head of government: Premier

Lawmaking body: Quango Renmin Daibiao Dahui or National People's Congress (NPC)

Administrative divisions: 23 provinces, five autonomous regions, and four municipalities

Independence: October 1, 1949

National symbol: Tian'anmen Gatetower with five stars above and a gear wheel below, encircled with ears of grain, is the country's emblem.

Geography

Total Area: 3,838,784 square miles (9,596,960 square kilometers)

Climate: Extremely diverse; tropical in south to subarctic in north

Highest point: Mount Everest, 29,205 feet (8,850 meters)

Lowest point: Turpan Basin, 508 feet (154 meters) below sea level

Major rivers: Yangtze, Huang He (Yellow), Amur, Yalu, Chang Jiang

Major landforms: Greater Khingan Range, Tian Shan Range, Altai Shan Range, Kunlin Shan Range, Qulian Shan Range, Himalayan Range, Gobi Range; Plateau of Tibet, Yunnan Plateau; Taklimakan Desert

Economy

Currency: Yuan, also referred to as the renminbi

Population below poverty line: 10%

Major natural resources: Coal, iron ore, petroleum, natural gas, mercury, tin, tungsten, antimony, manganese, molybdenum, vanadium, magnetite, aluminum, lead, zinc, uranium, hydropower potential

Major agricultural products: Rice, wheat, potatoes, corn, peanuts, tea, millet, barley, apples, cotton, oilseed, pork, fish

Major exports: Plastics, optical and medical equipment, computers and computer equipment, petroleum

Major imports: Machinery and equipment, oil and mineral fuels, metals, organic chemicals, cars

Historical Timeline

Buddhism spreads to
China from India during
the Han dynasty

During the Ming dynasty,
the Great Wall is built by
joining four earlier walls,
the capital moves to
Beijing, and the Forbidden
City is built

During the Sui dynasty,
the empire of China
reunites and the Grand
Canal is completed

 British colonies
are established in
North America

| 221 B.C. | A.D. 206–220 | 250 | 581–618 | 800 | 1271–1368 | 1368–1644 | 1600's |

King Zheng unifies the
Chinese empire and starts
the Qin dynasty; he calls
himself "Shihuang Di," or
"first emperor"

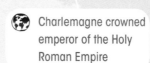 Charlemagne crowned
emperor of the Holy
Roman Empire

Emperor Kublai Khan
moves the court to
Beijing, appoints the
Italian explorer Marco
Polo to a court position,
and extends the Grand
Canal during the
Yuan dynasty

 The Maya rise to
prominence in
Central America

   Historical World Event

Chinese peasants rebel against
their rulers during the 14-year
Taiping Rebellion; about
20 million people are killed

Civil war rages in China
between the Nationalists,
led by Chiang Kai-shek, and
the Communists, led by
Mao Tse-tung

Civil war resumes with
the Communists winning;
they establish the People's
Republic of China led by
Mao Tse-tung in 1949;
Chinese Nationalists flee
to Taiwan

 The Korean War

 World War I

1839–1842 1850–1864 1911 1914–1918 1934–1937 1937 1939–1945 1946–1948 1950–1953

Nationalists led by Sun
Yat-sen overthrow the
Qing dynasty; they
set up a republic the
following year

During World War II,
Chinese unite to
oppose the invading
Japanese, who kill
20 million Chinese
before their defeat

China loses the Opium Wars
with Britain and is forced to
allow British merchants to
trade in China

Japanese attack and
invade China

Historical Timeline

Mao launches the Cultural Revolution, calling on students to rebel against authority and form units of Red Guards who brutally punish intellectuals, educators, and others

Qinghai-Tibet railway line, the world's highest train route, begins operating

SARS (severe acute respiratory syndrome) outbreak begins in China, sparking worldwide fears

 The Soviet Union collapses

1958–1960	1966–1976	1976	1991	1997	2001	2002–2003	2006

 Terrorist attacks on the two World Trade Center Towers in New York City and on the Pentagon in Washington, D.C., leave thousands dead

Mao's "Great Leap Forward" plan for collective farming fails, causing a famine that kills 30 million people

Deng Xiaoping dies; Jiang Zemin takes over; Hong Kong reverts to Chinese control and Macao follows the next year

Mao Tse-tung dies; Deng Xiaoping takes over as leader and re-establishes communication and trade with foreign countries, aiming for economic prosperity and modernization of China

Glossary

acupuncture | the stimulation of certain points in the body by penetrating the skin with metal needles

compulsory | something that is required

dialects | forms of a language that is spoken in a particular area or by a particular group of people

dynasty | succession of rulers from the same family; a powerful family or group of people whose members retain their power and influence through several generations

fall equinox | the time when the sun crosses Earth's equator, making day and night the same length of time; also called autumn equinox

gross domestic product | the total value of all goods and services produced by a country during a specific period

imperial | involving or relating to an empire or its ruler

impoverished | having little money or few possessions

literacy rate | the percentage of the population 15 years and older who can read and write

migrants | people who move regularly in order to find work, especially in harvesting crops

poverty level | the level of income below which one cannot afford to buy the things necessary to live

Western | located in or relating to Europe and North and South America

wok | large bowl-shaped cooking utensil used especially in stir-frying

Additional Resources

IN THE LIBRARY

DuTemple, Lesley A. *The Great Wall of China*. Minneapolis: Lerner Publications, 2003.

Jiang, Ji-Li. *Red Scarf Girl: A Memoir of the Cultural Revolution*. New York: HarperCollins Publishers, 1997.

Luh, Shu Shin. *The People of China*. Philadelphia: Mason Crest Publishers, 2006.

Ma, Yan. *The Diary of Ma Yan: The Struggles and Hopes of a Chinese Schoolgirl*. Edited by Pierre Haski and translated by Lisa Appignanesi. New York: Harper Collins, 2005.

O'Connor, Jane. *The Emperor's Silent Army: Terracotta Warriors of Ancient China*. New York: Viking, 2002.

Shane, C.J. *China*. San Diego: Greenhaven Press, 2003.

ON THE WEB

For more information on this topic, use FactHound.
1. Go to www.facthound.com
2. Type in this book ID: 0756520606
3. Click on the *Fetch It* button.

Look for more Global Connections books.

Teens in Australia
Teens in Brazil
Teens in France
Teens in India
Teens in Israel
Teens in Japan
Teens in Kenya

Teens in Mexico
Teens in Russia
Teens in Saudi Arabia
Teens in Spain
Teens in Venezuela
Teens in Vietnam

Source Notes

Page 42, line 17: "Shared Belief in the Golden Rule." ReligiousTolerance.org 2 Sept. 2006. 30 Nov. 2006. www.religioustolerance.org/reciproc.htm

Page 42, line 25: "Confucius Quotes." BrainyQuote. 2006. 30 Nov. 2006. www.brainyquote.com/quotes/authors/c/confucius.html

Page 65, column 2, line 9: Constitution of the People's Republic of China. 4 Dec. 1982. 28 Nov. 2006. http://english.people.com.cn/constitution/constitution.html

Page 79, line 6: Sara Naumann. *Visiting Hangzhou—China's Paradise on Earth*. About: China for Visitors. 27 Nov. 2006. http://gochina.about.com/od/cityareaguidesinchina/a/VisitHZ.htm

Page 84–85, At a Glance: United States. Central Intelligence Agency. *The World Factbook—China*. 16 Nov. 2006. 29 Nov. 2006. www.cia.gov/cia/publications/factbook/geos/ch.html

Select Bibliography

"Basic Education in China." *Ministry of Education of the People's Republic of China.* 3 July 2006. www.moe.edu.cn/english/

Beech, Hannah. "Bringing the Best and Brightest Back Home." *Time Asia.* 3 July 2006. www.time.com/time/asia/features/youngchina/t.pioneering.park.html

The Central People's Government of the People's Republic of China. 15 Aug. 2006. http://english.gov.cn/

Chin, Elizabeth, Marson Meyers, and Emma Wilson. "China: A Cultural Profile." *Citizenship and Immigration Canada.* 6 July 2006. www.cp-pc.ca/english/china/china_eng.pdf

China Education and Research Network. 10 Aug. 06. www.edu.cn/HomePage/english/index.shtml

"China to Build High-Speed Railways Next Year." *China Daily.* 16 Dec. 2004. 3 July 2006. www.chinadaily.com/cn/english/doc

Ebrey, Patricia Buckley. "A Visual Sourcebook of Chinese Civilization." University of Washington. 6 July 2006. http://depts.washington.edu/chinaciv/home/3intrhme.htm

Embassy of the United States Beijing. 11 Aug. 2006. http://beijing.usembassy-china.org.cn/

Frankenstein, Paul. "Condensed China: Chinese History for Beginners." 16 July 2006. http://asterius.com/china/index.html

Gunde, Richard. *Culture and Customs of China.* Westport, Conn.: Greenwood Press, 2002.

Li, Jianguo. "Will Traditional Festivals Disappear?" *Beijing Review*. 26 Jan. 2006. 17 July 2006. www.bjreview.com.cn/

Liu, Shinan. "Improved Educational Standards Required." *China Daily*. 7 June 2006. 2 July 2006. www.chinadaily.com.cn//cndy/2006-06/07/content_610122.htm

People's Daily Online. Xinhua News Agency. 4 July 2006. http://english.people.com.cn/

Robinson, Susan Porter. "Higher Education in China: The Next Superpower is Coming of Age." *American Council on Education*. 2 July 2006. www.acenet.edu/AM/Template.cfm?Section=Home&TEMPLATE=/CM/ContentDisplay.cfm&CONTENTID=11822

Sedgwick, Robert and Xiao Chen. "Education in China." *World Education News and Reviews*. 17 July 2006. www.wes.org/ewenr/02march/practical.htm

"Shanghai Nights." *Frontline World*. Public Broadcasting Service (PBS). 17 July 2006. www.pbs.org/frontlineworld/stories/china/facts.html

Stanat, Michael. *China's Generation Y: Understanding the Future Leaders of the World's Next Superpower*. Paramus, N.J.: Homa & Sekey Books, 2005.

Temple, Robert K.G. *The Genius of China: 3,000 Years of Science Discovery, and Invention*. New York: Simon and Schuster, 1986.

Tsutsui, William. "Confucius." University of Kansas. 20 June 2006. www.continuinged.ku.edu/isc/previews/hist640/lesson2.html

United States. Central Intelligence Agency. *The World Factbook—China*. 16 Nov. 2006. 29 Nov. 2006. www.cia.gov/cia/publications/factbook/geos/ch.html

United States. Library of Congress. Federal Research Division. *A Country Study: China*. February 2005. 6 July 2006. http://lcweb2.loc.gov/frd/cs/cntoc.html

Wilhelm, Richard. Translated by George H. Danton. *Confucius and Confucianism*. Port Washington, N.Y.: Kennikat Press, 1970.

"The World's Youth: 2006 Data Sheet." Population Reference Bureau, 2006. 25 June 2006. www.prb.org/pdf06/WorldsYouth2006DataSheet.pdf

Index

About the Author
Karen Conyers

As a writer, Karen Conyers has always had an interest in people and what makes them the way they are. The mother of two teenage boys, she has first-hand knowledge of teens and their interests. In 2004 she began working on a master's degree in English/technical communication.

About the Content Adviser
Cynthia Ning, Ph.D.

Our adviser for *Teens in China*, Dr. Ning serves as the associate director of the Center for Chinese Studies at the University of Hawaii. She regularly presents a wide range of lectures on Chinese culture. One of Dr. Ning's more unique research interests includes Chinese comic literature.

border to border • teen to teen • border to border • teen to teen • border to border